THREE CAPE COD

BOTANICAL WALKS IN

YARMOUTH, MA

Gary R. Sanford, Ph.D.

ISBN: 9798674725367

CONTENTS

PREFACE

This is the second in a series of booklets designed to provide habitat information, and a plant check list of common or conspicuous plants present along town conservation area trails. The first, "Three Cape Cod Botanical Walks In Dennis, MA", dealt with Princess Beach, Indian Lands, and Flax Pond Conservation Areas. In this booklet, conservation areas in Yarmouth are considered.

INTRODUCTION

This booklet provides checklists of common and conspicuous plants growing along three trail systems located in, and maintained by, the town of Yarmouth, MA. Details on plant ecology, topography, soils, and wetlands are also included. Trails are within the Horse Pond, Bud Carter, and Sandy Pond conservation areas, which are open and free to the public. They traverse a variety of landscape features that include nearly level to steep slopes, swales, depressions, cranberry bogs, ponds, streams, and freshwater wetlands. Walking is easy, and chances are that not more than one or two people will find their way past you during an outing.

The checklists offer a challenge to spot the presence of each species, as well as an aid in species identification. Beyond this, relationships between plants, plant communities, and landscape features can be explored. Plants occur in spatial patterns for a multitude of reasons, including the species reproductive strategy, phenotypic plasticity (changes in morphology or physiology in response to environmental conditions), physiological tolerance ranges, competitive ability, and the recurrence of similar environments within a landscape. For example, sweet pepperbush (*Clethra alnifolia L.*) grows in clumps because of its ability to reproduce by root suckering. The dense thickets of this shrub offer a competitive advantage that excludes many plants, and its ability to live in waterlogged soils results in a recurring pattern of occurrence in wetlands across the landscape.

Environmental conditions to keep in mind include severity of slope and the direction it is facing, position on slope, presence of depressions or swales, distance from water bodies, distance from salt water, potential to receive salt water spray, depth to groundwater, flooding or signs of past flooding, and soil characteristics. Plant growth is affected by localized weather conditions. Examples include: distance to the ocean which can affect growing season, location on slope which can affect the number of frost free days, and exposure which can affect plant desiccation from wind or ice.

Plant habit is important. Size and height affect availability of light. Shoot density affects competitive ability as well as successful reproductive strategies. Root morphology affects access to water and nutrients. Natural root grafting can enhance access to water and nutrients, and potentially result in the transfer of organic compounds between plants.

Another important consideration is the occurrence of past perturbations. Historically, most of the Cape was logged and placed in agriculture. Most agriculture has since been abandoned, and our forests are still recovering. Fire has played an important role in our landscape, as well as disease and insect infestations.

One of the most important and generally the easiest environmental condition to spot is the presence of wetlands. Different species have different affinities for wetlands. The checklists include species wetland status in the northeast. They are classified as one of the following: obligate, facultative wetland, facultative, facultative upland, and upland. Appendix 1 provides definitions for these groupings.

Each trail description includes discussions of topography, soils, and wetlands. Portions of USGS quadrangles provide information on hills and depressions. Orthophotographs (aerial photographs that have been adjusted so that scale is uniform across the image) show characteristics of vegetation, and the location of wetlands. After each checklist, a brief ecological examination of one or two species is provided.

Down-loading trail maps from the town website is encouraged. It is a good idea to know how to identify poison ivy when walking on any trail on Cape Cod.   Protection against ticks is also recommended.

Gary R. Sanford

PLANT IDENTIFICATION

If you are not able to identify many of the common plant species growing on the Cape, it is suggested that an identification manual be brought along on your walk, and utilized as seen fit. The following approach can help ID a specimen by restricting your focus to just a few species, thus narrowing down your search. In addition, it will sharpen your observation skills relative to ecological conditions.

Identify Your Relative Environmental Position

Look at the surrounding topography. Are you on top of a large hill, on a slope, near the bottom of a slope, or in a flat area or depression with signs of flooding? Is the terrain dominated by hills and depressions? If so, are you in the depression or on the hill? What direction does the slope face?

Water availability is one predominant characteristic that determines local plant distributions. The least amount of water will be located on top of a hill or its slope. Groundwater flow generally follows topographic gradients (there are localized exceptions), and groundwater level will be found closer to the surface near the toe of a slope. Often it will reach near the surface in low flat areas and depressions. Side slope springy areas are also a possibility, but given Cape soil conditions, are not often found here. South and west facing slopes are generally drier than north and east facing slopes. Swales and depressions accumulate more water than adjacent slopes. Observations on the relative water availability, in conjunction with the wetland status (see Appendix 1) of listed species, can suggest possible candidates in the identification process.

Wetland or Upland?

Decide if the plant is located in a wetland or upland. Flooded areas are obviously going to be wetlands, however areas which are only temporarily flooded, or simply have groundwater near the surface for periods of time, are common wetland types. These wetlands will often have a dense thick shrub layer that reaches a height of 6 feet (2 m) or more. Upland shrubs are often only a few feet high, and occupy sites higher on a slope than wetlands. There are many exceptions to these plant height generalizations. Typically, wetlands will have a lush appearance compared to nearby uplands.

Determine Growth Habit

Growth habit simply refers to the life form of a plant. The USDA system (see Appendix 2) is used in trail checklists (Tables 1, 2 & 3). Within checklists, species are grouped by their growth habit, and, within each grouping, arranged by their wetland status. Plants growing in uplands include "upland" and "facultative upland" species. Those found in wetlands include "facultative wetland" and "obligate" species. "Facultative" species are often found in both upland and wetland conditions.

Once determinations concerning location (upland versus wetland), and growth habit are reached, select a representative specimen for identification. Evaluate species listed in the chosen grouping to determine the specimen's identity. Keep in mind two things. The tables are not intended to be complete floristic lists, but simply represent common and conspicuous plants observed on the trails. Your plant may not be on the list. Also, the vast majority of species can be found both in uplands or wetlands. Evaluate other candidates based upon their wetland indicator status.

As a hypothetical example, consider the top of a hill that is dominated by trees. Shrub growth is limited to plants only a few feet high. Clearly, this is an upland. Select a specimen tree for identification, and then examine the trail list for species catalogued as upland or facultative upland trees. In this example, we can imagine six listed tree species. Four of them are broad-leaved plants, and these can be eliminated immediately because your specimen is a needle-leaved evergreen. Use your manual to choose between the remaining two species (or read further).

8

UPLAND OAKS AND PINES

Across the Cape, you will see oaks and pines as dominant trees, so here are some characteristics helpful in identifying a few of these species.

Pitch pine (*Pinus rigida*) can easily be identified from its needle clusters (fascicles), each of which contain three needles that can reach 5 inches (13 cm) in length. Mature tree bark consists of thick flat plates and deep furrows, and sprouts of needles may often be seen growing on the trunk. Female cones are from 2 to 4 inches (5 to 10 cm) long; a short, stout prickle develops on each cone scale.

White pine (*Pinus strobus*) is often conspicuous by its large size, commonly over 100 feet (30 m) tall, and can even reach 150 feet (46 m) in height. Mature trees are branch-free on the lower boles, and the thick bark has scaly long ridges with furrows. The five needle fascicles that are up to 5 inches (13 cm) long make it easy to identify. Both male and female cones appear on the same tree, and the female cones grow to between 4 and 7 inches (10 and 18 cm) in length.

Oak trees fall into two categories here on the Cape, red and white. Both groups have variable shaped leaves with sinuses (indentations between lobes) ranging from deep to shallow. Sometimes the full range of leaf shapes exist on the same tree; shallow sinuses can occur in shade while deep sinuses develop in full sun. The tips of leaf lobes are smooth in the white oak group, while species in the red oak group have bristle-tipped lobes.

Within the white oak group, **white oak** (*Quercus alba*) is very common on the Cape. This slow growing species can reach heights of 60 to 80 feet (18 to 24 m). The plant has 4 to 7 inch (10 to 18 cm) long leaves with smooth lobe tips, and the bark is distinctive. Bark has a grayish light color, and is scaly on small stems but irregularly platy or blocky on larger trunks.

Within the red oak group of trees, black oak, red oak, and scarlet oak should be mentioned. They are harder to identify than the smooth-leafed white oak, and, since they hybridize, often have intermediate forms. Try to use more than one characteristic.

Black oak (*Quercus velutina*) is a medium-sized, deciduous tree that will usually grow to about 60 to 80 feet (18 to 24 m). The leaves, with 5 to 9 bristle-tipped lobes, can vary from 4 to 10 inches (10 to 25 cm) in length. Glossy leafs have undersides covered in pubescence (downy hairs) that is shed in late summer; buds are entirely covered with a light colored pubescence, and acorn cups have loose scales that stick out near the top of the cup. The nearly black bark of mature trees is thick with deep vertical furrows, and has horizontal breaks.

Northern red oak (*Quercus rubra*) is a medium to large tree, and will usually grow to about 65 to 100 feet (20-30 m) in height. Leaves can range from 4 ¾ to 8 inches (12 to 20 cm) in length, and have 7 to 11 bristle-tipped lobes. Sinuses reach less than half the distance from lobe tips to the midrib. Look for smooth reddish petioles (leaf stalks). Underside of leaf ranges from gray to light yellowish-green in color with short tufts of wooly hair in the axils of veins.   Acorn cups are shallow, and have reddish-brown pubescent (hairy) scales with dark margins. The pointed ovoid buds have chestnut-brown pubescent scales. Mature tree bark is dark gray to black with shallow vertical furrows separating light colored scaly ridges. Ridges usually reach within 1 to 2 feet (.3 to . 6 m) of the ground.

Scarlet oak (*Quercus coccinea*) is a relatively short-lived, but fast growing, deciduous tree that usually grows 60 to 80 feet (18-24 m) tall. It frequently has downward arching branches and an enlarged trunk base.   Leaves can range from 2 ¾ to 6 ¼ inches (7 to 16 cm) in length and have 5 to 9 bristle-tipped lobes. Sinuses nearly reach the midrib (more than half-way from lobe end), and lobes are distally expanded. Leaves are shiny light green above, and have tufts of hair in the axils of veins underneath. Acorn cups are glossy dark reddish-brown, and cover ⅓ to ½ of the nut. Terminal buds clustered at ends of branches are reddish-brown with pubescence near apices.   Tree bark has shallow vertical furrows separating light colored scaly ridges. Ridges usually stop 6 to 12 feet (2 to 4 m) above the ground.

Gary R. Sanford

HORSE POND
CONSERVATION AREA

Trail through Water Department Land leading to Horse Pond.

Horse Pond is located in Yarmouth about 1.5 miles (2.4 km) north-east of Lewis Bay, and 2.0 miles (3.2 km) north by north-west of Nantucket Sound. Cape Cod Bay lies 3.5 miles (5.6 km) north of the pond. Horse Pond Conservation Area (see Figure 1) borders the northern shore of the Pond; Yarmouth Water Department land extends west, north, and east of the Conservation Area. Access is off of Higgins Crowell Road just north of Buck Island Road.

The access trail runs east through Water Department land, and crosses an unpaved road (Horse Pond Road) before continuing on to the Horse Pond Conservation Area. A loop walk can be made by hiking through the Conservation Area, then turning north and, ultimately, west to follow Horse Pond Road back to the access trail. The Conservation Area together with the Water Department land shown in Figure 1 total a little over 110 acres, and are both considered in the following material.

As with the rest of the Cape, the site owes its form and geology from the Pleistocene glaciation. It lies within Harwich outwash plain deposits which are mostly gravelly sand with localized deposits of silt and clay. Much of the landscape is relatively flat with elevations varying 20 or so feet across the site. Horse Pond is located at the lowest elevation just below the 20-foot contour. Topographic diversity is added with the presence of both wet and dry kettle holes, and a number of these kettle holes are shown on Figure 1. They were formed from blocks of glacial ice that became surrounded with sediments. Upon melting, depressions were left in the landscape. The bottoms of some depressions are above the existing water table and remain dry, other bottoms are at or near the water table resulting in wetlands, and finally, some are well below the water table and are best described as ponds.

Four ponds are shown on the USGS map (Figure 1). (Note that the Figure is oriented so that north is to the left.) The larger pond to the south is Horse Pond. A small portion of Bassets Lot Pond is shown encroaching from the east; two small unnamed ponds are north of Horse Pond, one of which is boot shaped. This latter pond was without standing water in the fall of 2019 and summer of 2020.

The Natural Resources Conservation Service has mapped Carver coarse sand, and Freetown and Swansea muck soils on site. Carver coarse sand, an upland soil, covers about 90% of the site, while the Freetown and Swansea mucks occur in wetlands.

About 17% of the uplands have nearly level Carver soils (0 to 3% slopes), roughly 55% of the Carver unit occurs on gently sloping land (3 to 8% slopes), and about 28% occupies strongly sloping sites (8 to 15% slopes). The Carver unit is composed of deep coarse-textured soil that is excessively well drained, and has very rapid permeabilities both in the subsoil and substratum. Soil water holding capacity is low, and depth to the seasonal high groundwater table exceeds 6 feet (2 m). Carver soils tend to be droughty, and, as a result, seedling mortality may be exacerbated.

The "Soil Survey of Barnstable County, Massachusetts"

identifies the most common trees on Carver soil as pitch pine, scrub oak, and white oak, and states: "Generally, these trees are of poor quality and seldom attain heights of more than 25 feet."

Freetown soil has muck and peat to a depth of 65 inches (1.65 m) or more; Swansea soil has muck to a depth of about 35 inches (.9 m). Muck is highly decomposed organic matter; peat is largely undecomposed organic matter. These soils are similar in having moderate or moderately rapid permeabilities in the organic layers, very high water holding capacity, and seasonal high water tables at or near the surface for most of the year.

DEP has mapped five wetland areas on the site as shown in Figure 2. The first is south of the access trail between Higgins Crowell Road and the unpaved Horse Pond Road. It occupies a depression without an inlet or outlet, and has been classified as a deciduous wooded swamp.

After crossing the unpaved road, the access trail continues through oak/pitch pine woods with black huckleberry (*Gaylussacia baccata*) and lowbush blueberry (*Vaccinium angustifolium* and *V. pallidum*) ground cover. It takes a turn to the south along a deep marsh that connects to Horse Pond. The trail continues east to a "rotary" (see Figure 2B). An isolated wetland classified as a shrub swamp is located about 200 feet (61 m) north-west of this rotary.

The remaining wetlands are associated with the two unnamed ponds. DEP has classified the wetland around the boot shaped pond as a deciduous wooded swamp. DEP shows no open water within the remaining ponding area, but does show an inner deep marsh surrounded by a deciduous wooded swamp.

Horse Pond and the two unnamed ponds are shallow. The ground water driven pond levels fluctuate not only seasonally, but also vary between wet and dry precipitation years. According to the town trail map, the neighboring town wells also play a role in lowering pond levels. As pond levels decline over the summer, large expanses of pond bottom become exposed. The periodically exposed portions offer an environment conducive to the growth of sedges, rushes, quillworts, sundews, and, as noted by the trail map, certain rare species, such as Plymouth Gentian (*Sabatia kennedyana*). The recurrent re-flooding of these shelves and pond bottoms is important to keep adjacent woody vegetation from encroaching into and displacing wet meadow/marsh vegetation.

Wooded wetlands have a tree canopy of red maple (*Acer rubrum*) and tupelo (*Nyssa sylvatica*), and an understory of sweet pepperbush (*Clethra alnifolia*) and highbush blueberry *(Vaccinium corymbosum)*. Vegetation adjacent to the ponds is often dominated by shrubs, including sweet pepperbush, leatherleaf (*Chamaedaphne calyculata*), and sweet gale *(Myrica gale)*. Leatherleaf and sweet gale are bog plants which do well in the peaty/mucky soils.

Upland vegetation consists of a mixed oak pine woods (see Figure 2) that includes scarlet oak (*Quercus coccinea*), northern red oak (*Quercus rubra*), white oak (*Quercus alba*), and pitch pine (*Pinus rigida*).

The trail passes along the edge of a large treeless patch on the site's eastern side (see Figure 2C). A recent fire has claimed the pitch pine. Numerous scarlet oak sprouts from basal buds have produced three or four foot shoots. An occasional pitch pine seedling is present, but by-in-large, ground cover, that includes black huckleberry, lowbush blueberry, wintergreen, and brackenfern, predominate as of this writing.

Table 1 lists common or conspicuous plant species observed along the trails. In order to discourage damage to rare species habitat from trampling or collecting, wet meadow/marsh species are not included in this table.

Figure 1.   Portion of USGS quadrangle showing Horse Pond Conservation Area.   Contour interval = 10 ft.   Quadrangle from Bureau of Geographic Information, Commonwealth of Massachusetts, Executive Office of Technology and Security Services. Trails and boundaries from Town of Yarmouth Trail Map.

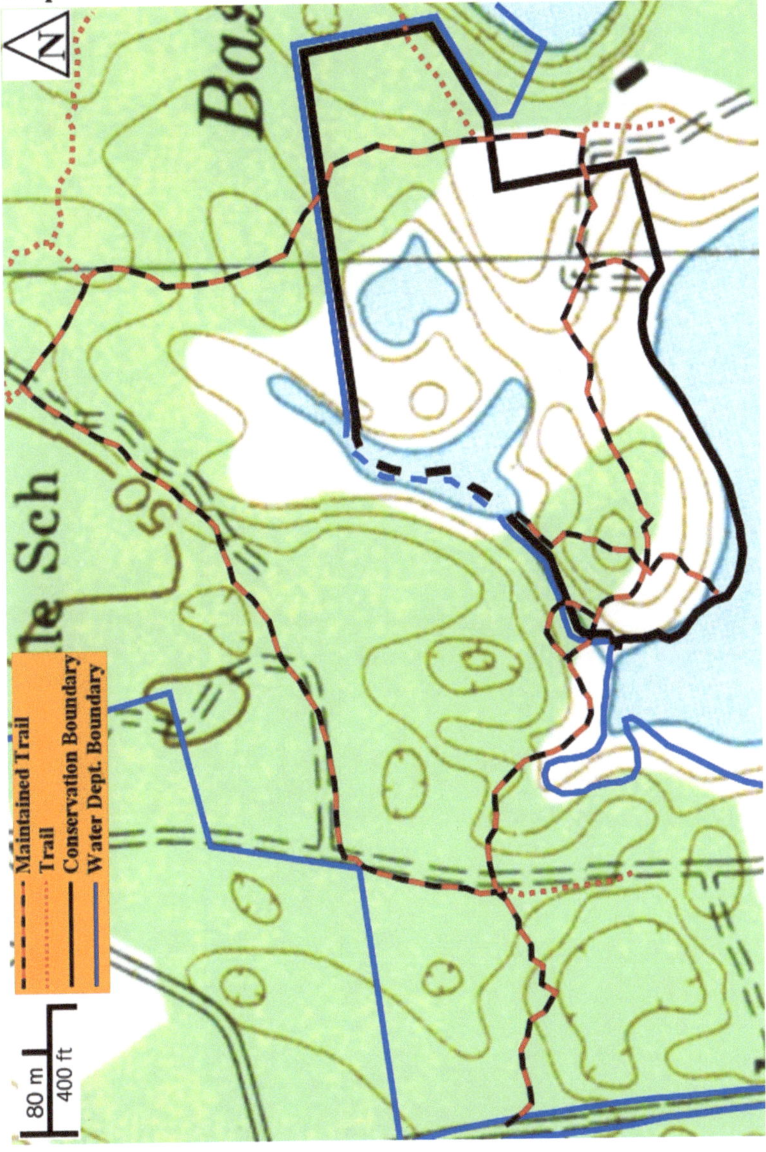

Figure 2A. Orthophotograph of Horse Pond Conservation Area. DEP wetland boundary from Bureau of Geographic Information, Commonwealth of Massachusetts, Executive Office of Technology and Security Services. Trails and other boundaries from Town of Yarmouth Trail Map.

Figure 2B. Orthophotograph of Horse Pond Conservation Area. DEP wetland boundary from Bureau of Geographic Information, Commonwealth of Massachusetts, Executive Office of Technology and Security Services. Trails and other boundaries from Town of Yarmouth Trail Map.

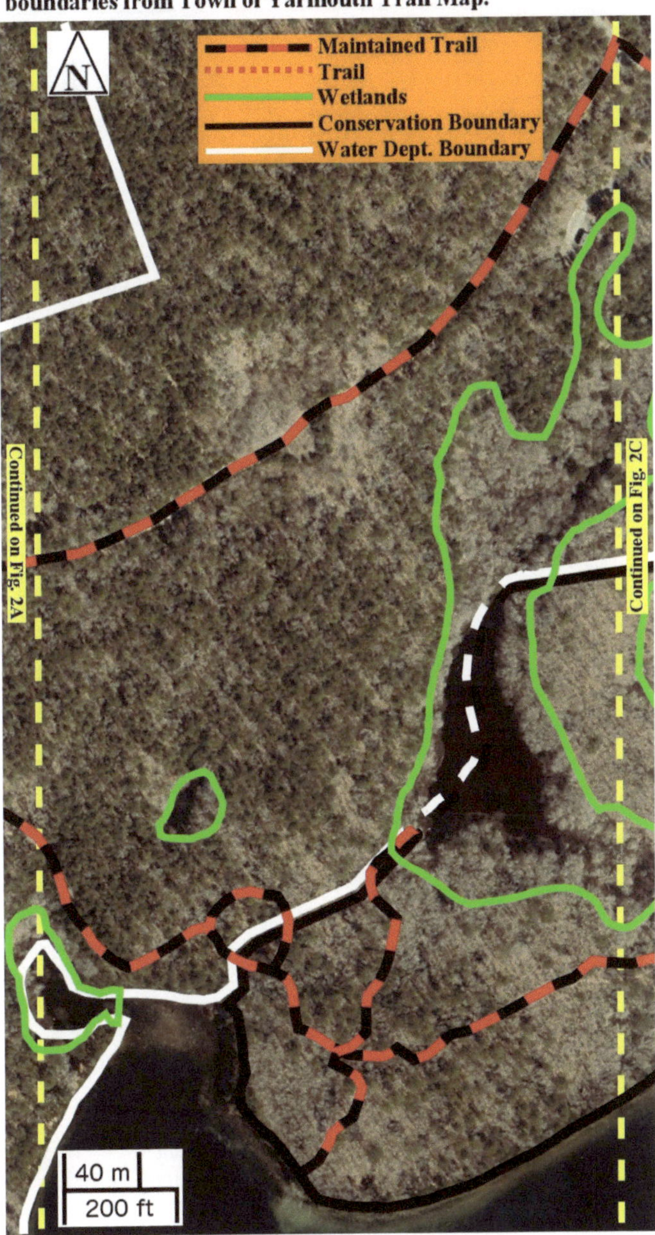

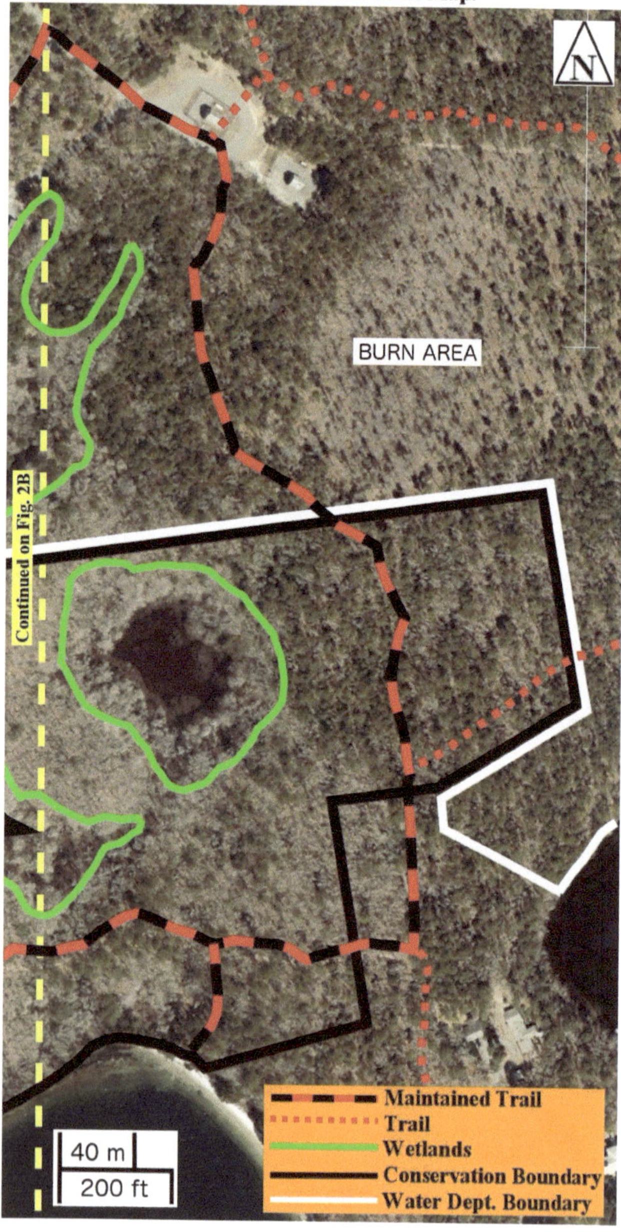

Figure 2C. Orthophotograph of Horse Pond Conservation Area. DEP wetland boundary from Bureau of Geographic Information, Commonwealth of Massachusetts, Executive Office of Technology and Security Services. Trails and other boundaries from Town of Yarmouth Trail Map.

Table 1. Checklist of species noted along Horse Pond Conservation Area trails.

✓	Scientific Name	Common Name	Wetland Status[1]	Growth Habit[2]
	Quercus coccinea Münchh.	scarlet oak	upland[3]	Tree
	Quercus velutina Lam.	black oak	upland[3]	Tree
	Pinus rigida Mill.	pitch pine	FACU	Tree
	Pinus strobus L.	eastern white pine	FACU	Tree
	Populus grandidentata Michx.	big-tooth aspen	FACU	Tree
	Quercus alba L.	white oak	FACU	Tree
	Quercus rubra L.	northern red oak	FACU	Tree
	Acer rubrum L.	red maple	FAC	Tree
	Nyssa sylvatica Marsh.	tupelo	FAC	Tree
	Quercus ilicifolia Wangenh.	bear oak	upland[3]	Shrub/Tree
	Prunus serotina Ehrh.	black cherry	FACU	Shrub/Tree
	Sassafras albidum (Nutt.) Nees.	sassafras	FACU	Shrub/Tree
	Gaylussacia baccata (Wangenh.) K. Koch	black huckleberry	FACU	Shrub
	Vaccinium stamineum L.	deerberry	FACU	Shrub
	Clethra alnifolia L.	sweet pepper bush	FAC	Shrub
	Kalmia angustifolia L.	sheep laurel	FAC	Shrub
	Morella pensylvanica (Mirbel) Kartesz	northern bayberry	FAC	Shrub/Tree

✓	Scientific Name	Common Name	Wetland Status[1]	Growth Habit[2]
	Smilax rotundifolia L.	horsebrier	FAC	Shrub/Vine
	Eubotrys racemosus (L.) Nutt.	swamp doghobble; Fetterbush	FACW	Shrub
	Ilex glabra (L.) Gray	inkberry	FACW	Shrub
	Rhododendron viscosum (L.) Torr.	swamp azalea	FACW	Shrub
	Vaccinium corymbosum L.	highbush blueberry	FACW	Shrub
	Viburnum nudum L. var. cassinoides (L.) Torr. & A. Gray	withe-rod	FACW	Shrub/Tree
	Chamaedaphne calyculata (L.) Moench.	leatherleaf	OBL	Shrub
	Myrica gale L. Show	sweetgale	OBL	Shrub
	Comptonia peregrina (L.) Coult.	sweet fern	upland[3]	Shrub/ Subshrub
	Vaccinium pallidum Aiton	early lowbush blueberry	upland[3]	Subshrub
	Gaultheria procumbens L.	wintergreen, eastern teaberry	FACU	Shrub/ Subshrub
	Vaccinium angustifolium Aiton	late lowbush blueberry	FACU	Shrub Subshrub
	Vaccinium macrocarpon Aiton	cranberry	OBL	Shrub Subshrub
	Aralia nudicaulis L.	wild sarsaparilla	FACU	Forb/herb/ Subshrub
	Pteridium aquilinum (L.) Kuhn	brackenfern	FACU	Forb/herb

✓	Scientific Name	Common Name	Wetland Status[1]	Growth Habit[2]
	Trientalis borealis Raf.	starflower	FAC	Forb/herb
	Lycopodiella inundata (L.) Holub	inundated clubmoss	OBL	Forb/herb Subshrub
	Carex pensylvanica Lam	Pennsylvania sedge	upland[3]	Graminoid
	Sphagnum L.	sphagnum	wetland	Nonvascular
	Celastrus orbiculatus Thunb.	oriental bittersweet	UPL	Vine

[1]See Appendix 1 [2]See Appendix 2. [3]Not listed on the National Wetland Plant List.

Additional Ecological Information: Leatherleaf

Leatherleaf (*Chamaedaphne calyculata*) is a shrub that forms dense thickets, and reaches heights of 4.9 ft (1.5 m). The many branched shoot system has twigs covered in tiny brownish scales. Underground horizontal shoots (rhizomes) reach an average depth within organic substrates of about a foot (31 cm). Alternate evergreen leaves are tough; they are oblong to elliptic, 0.6-2 in (1.5-5 cm) long, and finely toothed. The leaf undersides are covered in tiny brownish scales giving the plant undersurface a brownish coloration. In early spring, the plant produces small white urn-shaped flowers along one side of terminal inflorescences. Flowers produce a woody, gray capsule that can persist through the winter.

Leatherleaf is circumboreal, extending southward through the northeastern U.S. and the Lake States. We usually associate leatherleaf, an obligate species, with sphagnum bogs, but it also grows along lake and stream margins, kettle pond edges, and in wet peat. Its growth substrate is generally wet and acidic (less than pH 5).

When growing in bogs, it is the first species to gain a foothold in the Sphagnum mat, growing right up to waters edge, and is important in extending the bog mat. It persists within the mature and late stages of bog succession. However, it is shade intolerant, and thins as tall shrubs and trees develop. Leatherleaf tolerates low nutrient conditions.

The species reproduces vegetatively via its rhizomes. Sexual reproduction results in a seed set from open-pollinated flowers that can range up to 95%, but self-fertilized flowers produce low seed set. Seeds will germinate after cold stratification.

Leatherleaf may persist in bogs over prolonged periods, partly because of its ability to regenerate after fire. Its ability to survive fire is probably related to the location of rhizomes deep in water saturated substrates.

BUD CARTER
CONSERVATION AREA

Trail entrance from North Dennis Road.

The Bud Carter Conservation area, located a little north of Route 6, is about 3 miles (4.8 km) south of Cape Cod Bay, and 3.3 miles (5.3 km) north of Nantucket Sound. North Dennis Road, West Road, and West Great Western Road form a rough triangle containing most of the Conservation Area. Access to the trail system is from both West Great Western Road, and North Dennis Road (see Figure 3). The areas within both the conservation land and the adjacent water department land, as shown on chapter figures, are considered in the following material.

The site occurs within Sandwich moraine deposits. These glacial deposits are composed mostly of sand and gravel with abundant fine sand, silt, and clay. Till (unsorted material deposited directly by glacial ice) and boulders may be found on top of stratified drift (water transported and sorted into distinct horizontal layers or bands).

Soils present include sand pits, Carver coarse sand, Barnstable sandy loam, Plymouth loamy coarse sand, and Nantucket sandy loam. The Natural Resources Conservation Service has mapped a soil complex consisting of Plymouth and Barnstable soils together, and a second complex consisting of Barnstable, Plymouth, and Nantucket soils, on the site. Complexes have soils that are intricately mixed or in very small areas, making individual mapping impractical. The general location of soils on site, and a comparison of soil characteristics is presented in Appendix 3.

The "Soil Survey of Barnstable County, Massachusetts" identifies the most common trees on Carver soil as pitch pine, scrub oak, and white oak, and states: "Generally, these trees are of poor quality and seldom attain heights of more than 25 feet."

The Plymouth-Barnstable complex is extremely bouldery, and consists of about 55% Plymouth soil, 20% Barnstable soil, and 25% other soils. The Barnstable-Plymouth-Nantucket complex is very bouldery, and includes about 35% Barnstable soil, 30% Plymouth soil, 20% Nantucket soil, and 15% other soils. The "Soil Survey" identifies the most common trees on either complex as pitch pine, white oak, scarlet oak, eastern white pine and black oak.

Moraine deposits have left an area of moderately rough terrain. Contour lines shown on Figure 3 range from 10 to 130 feet, and numerous crests and depressions are present. Paths are often narrow with many side paths leading to dead ends. However, loop trails, in conjunction with the main trail, (see Figure 3) provide ways to either shorten or lengthen an outing without back tracking.

Not counting the cranberry fields, DEP has mapped five small vegetated wetland areas on the site as shown in Figure 4. Three small patches scattered along the northern site border, and inaccessible by trail, have been classified as deciduous wooded swamps. Two others are located within the water department parcel. A deciduous wooded swamp is associated with the ponding area, and a scrub shrub swamp is located just west of the ponding area near the open sand pit, as shown in Figure 4B.

Although not identified by DEP, wetland vegetation is present beside the unnamed pond at the North Dennis Road entrance.

These plants can be viewed along the Bud Carter Memorial Trail. Look for red maple *(Acer rubrum)*, tupelo (*Nyssa sylvatica*), northern bayberry (*Morella pensylvanica*), sweet pepper bush (*Clethra alnifolia*), and highbush blueberry *(Vaccinium corymbosum)*.

The rolling and hilly terrain offers a variety of habitats. Look for white, scarlet, and black oaks (*Quercus alba, Q. coccinea, Q. velutina*). Pitch pine (*Pinus rigida*) is common. Occasional patches of inkberry (*Ilex glabra*) and sheep laurel (*Kalmia angustifolia*) are present, along with more extensive areas of lowbush blueberry (*Vaccinium angustifolium* and *V. pallidum*). Wintergreen (*Gaultheria procumbens*) is common. It should be noted that Figure 3 shows a large area in the northern portion of the site without woods (white area). The latest revision by the USGS map (unavailable on Mass GIS) shows this area as largely wooded, which is in agreement with Figure 4 (orthophotograph from 2019). Table 2 lists plant species observed along the trails.

Figure 3. Portion of USGS quadrangle showing part of the Bud Carter Conservation Area. Contour interval = 10 ft. Quadrangle from Bureau of Geographic Information, Commonwealth of Massachusetts, Executive Office of Technology and Security Services. Trails from Town of Yarmouth Trail Map.

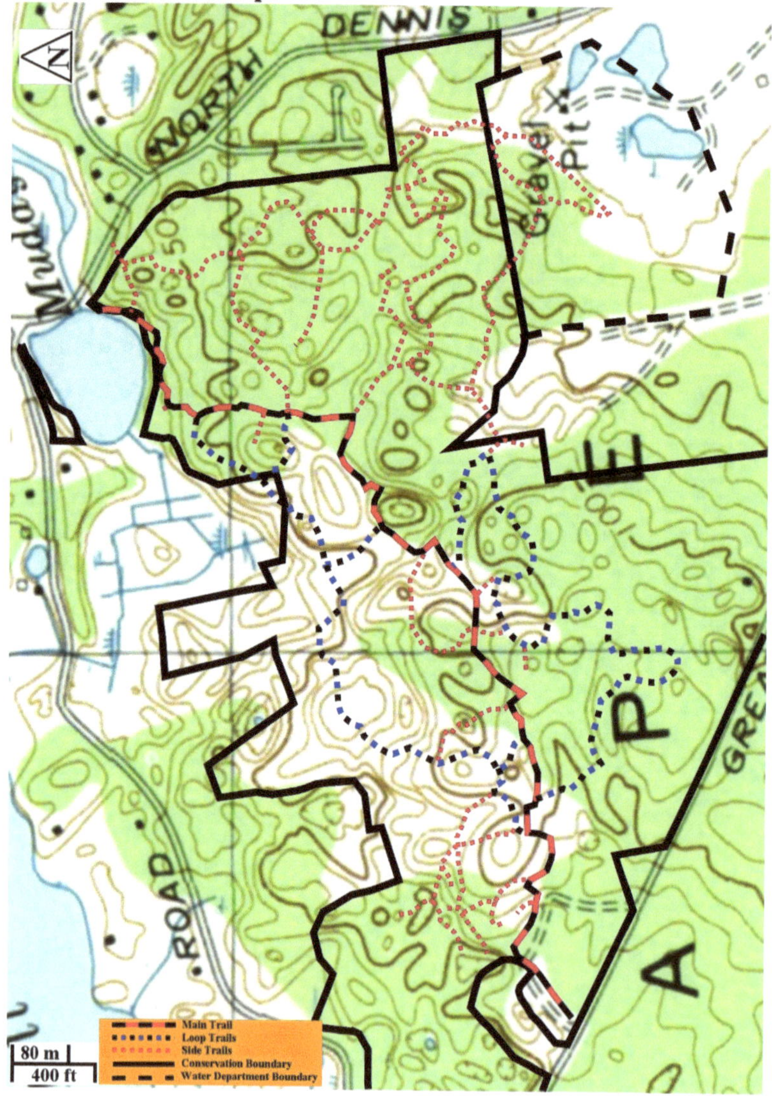

Figure 4A.   Orthophotograph of Bud Carter Conservation Area.   DEP wetland boundary from Bureau of Geographic Information, Commonwealth of Massachusetts, Executive Office of Technology and Security Services. Trails from Town of Yarmouth Trail Map.

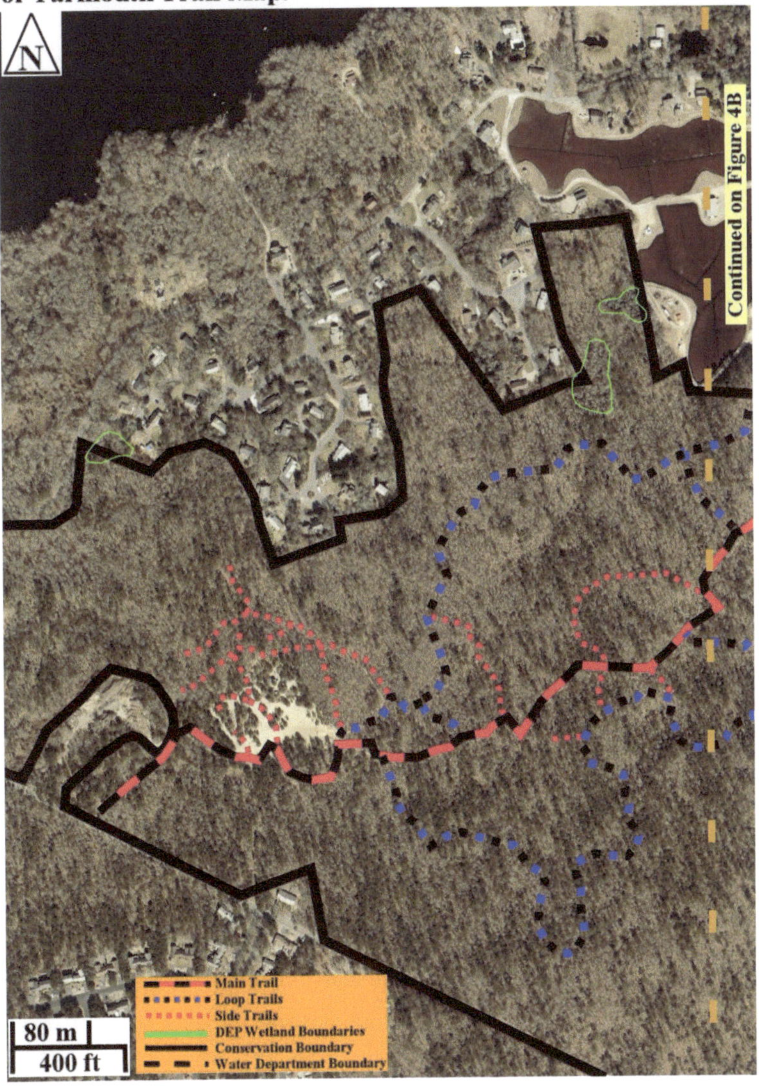

Figure 4B.   Orthophotograph of Bud Carter Conservation Area.   DEP wetland boundary from Bureau of Geographic Information, Commonwealth of Massachusetts, Executive Office of Technology and Security Services.   Trails from Town of Yarmouth Trail Map.

Table 2. Checklist of species noted along Bud Carter Conservation Area trails.

✔	Scientific Name	Common Name	Wetland Status[1]	Growth Habit[2]
	Quercus coccinea Münchh.	scarlet oak	upland[3]	Tree
	Quercus velutina Lam.	black oak	upland[3]	Tree
	Fagus grandifolia Ehrh.	American beech	FACU	Tree
	Pinus rigida Mill.	pitch pine	FACU	Tree
	Pinus strobus L.	eastern white pine	FACU	Tree
	Populus grandidentata Michx.	big-tooth aspen	FACU	Tree
	Quercus alba L.	white oak	FACU	Tree
	Robinia pseudoacacia L.	black locust	FACU	Tree
	Acer rubrum L.	red maple	FAC	Tree
	Betula populifolia Marshall	gray birch	FAC	Tree
	Nyssa sylvatica Marsh.	tupelo	FAC	Tree
	Quercus ilicifolia Wangenh.	bear oak	upland[3]	Shrub/Tree
	Rhus copallinum L.	winged sumac	UPL	Shrub/Tree
	Hamamelis virginiana L.	American witchhazel	FACU	Shrub/Tree
	Prunus serotina Ehrh.	black cherry	FACU	Shrub/Tree
	Sassafras albidum (Nutt.) Nees.	sassafras	FACU	Shrub/Tree

✔	Scientific Name	Common Name	Wetland Status[1]	Growth Habit[2]
	Morella pensylvanica (Mirbel) Kartesz	**northern bayberry**	**FAC**	**Shrub/Tree**
	Viburnum dentatum L.	**southern arrowwood**	**FAC**	**Shrub/Tree**
	Viburnum nudum L. var. cassinoides (L.) Torr. & A. Gray	**withe-rod**	**FACW**	**Shrub/Tree**
	Gaylussacia baccata (Wangenh.) K. Koch	**black huckleberry**	**FACU**	**Shrub**
	Vaccinium stamineum L.	**deerberry**	**FACU**	**Shrub**
	Clethra alnifolia L.	**sweet pepper bush**	**FAC**	**Shrub**
	Kalmia angustifolia L.	**sheep laurel**	**FAC**	**Shrub**
	Smilax rotundifolia L.	**horsebrier**	**FAC**	**Shrub/Vine**
	Eubotrys racemosus (L.) Nutt.	**swamp doghobble; Fetterbush**	**FACW**	**Shrub**
	Ilex glabra (L.) Gray	**inkberry**	**FACW**	**Shrub**
	Ilex verticillata (L.) Gray	**winterberry**	**FACW**	**Shrub**
	Rhododendron viscosum (L.) Torr.	**swamp azalea**	**FACW**	**Shrub**
✔	*Vaccinium corymbosum L.*	**highbush blueberry**	**FACW**	**Shrub**

✓	Scientific Name	Common Name	Wetland Status[1]	Growth Habit[2]
	Comptonia peregrina (L.) J.M. Coult.	sweet fern	upland[3]	Shrub/ Subshrub
	Vaccinium pallidum Aiton	early lowbush blueberry	upland[3]	Subshrub
	Gaultheria procumbens L.	wintergreen, eastern teaberry	FACU	Shrub/ Subshrub
	Rubus flagellaris Willd.	northern dewberry	FACU	Subshrub
	Vaccinium angustifolium Aiton	late lowbush blueberry	FACU	Shrub/ Subshrub
	Toxicodendron radicans (L.) Kuntze	eastern poison ivy	FAC	Forb/herb Shrub Subshrub Vine
	Dennstaedtia punctilobula (Michx.) T. Moore	hay scented fern	UPL	Forb/herb
	Aralia nudicaulis L.	wild sarsaparilla	FACU	Forb/herb Subshrub
	Maianthemum canadense Desf.	Canada mayflower	FACU	Forb/herb
	Phytolacca americana L.	pokeweed	FACU	Forb/herb
	Pteridium aquilinum (L.) Kuhn	brackenfern	FACU	Forb/herb
✓	*Trientalis borealis Raf.*	starflower	FAC	Forb/herb
	Cypripedium acaule Aiton	pink lady slipper	FACW	Forb/herb

✔	Scientific Name	Common Name	Wetland Status[1]	Growth Habit[2]
	Carex pensylvanica Lam	Pennsylvania sedge	upland[3]	Graminoid
	Celastrus orbiculatus Thunb.	oriental bittersweet	UPL	Vine

[1]See Appendix 1 [2]See Appendix 2. [3]Not listed on the National Wetland Plant List.

Additional Ecological Information: Black Oak

Black oak (*Quercus velutina*) is a medium-sized, deciduous tree that will usually grow to about 60 to 80 feet (18 to 24 m). The leaves, with 5 to 9 bristle-tipped lobes, can vary from 4 to 10 inches (10 to 25 cm) in length. Leaf shape varies with heavily shaded one's having shallow notches between lobes while leaves exposed to more sun develop deep notches. The glossy leafs have undersides covered in pubescence (downy hairs) that is shed in late summer; buds are entirely covered with a light colored pubescence, and acorn cups have loose scales that stick out near the top of the cup. The nearly black bark of mature trees is thick with deep vertical furrows, and has horizontal breaks.

Black oak and scarlet oak have variable and overlapping leaf morphologies, and they can hybridize so that individuals exist with intermediate characteristics. Look for a variety of identifiers including glossy leafs with hairy undersides, buds that are entirely covered with a light colored pubescence (downy hairs), and acorn cups with loose scales that stick out near the top of the cap

Both male and female flowers are inconspicuous, and appear separately on the same tree (monoecious). Clusters of male flowers occur in catkins, while one to four female flowers can be found together in a spike. Wind pollination occurs just before or with spring leaf-out, and like scarlet oak, acorns mature in two years, dropping in the fall and germinating the following spring.

The species is considered intermediate in shade tolerance, being more tolerant than black cherry, but less tolerant than white oak. Trees may reach 225 years in age, but most will live about 100 years. Without disturbance from fire, wind throw, or other damaging agents, black oak will be succeeded by more shade-tolerant trees.

Seeds are consistently produced each year, and good seed crops occur every 2 to 3 years, however, because of seed consumption by insects and wildlife, a high percentage of seeds are damaged. Local seed dispersal is accomplished by gravity, squirrels, and mice, while longer distance dispersal can be done by blue jays.

Seed germination is favored by being in contact with or buried in mineral soil and covered by a light litter layer. Seeds exposed on top of the litter may dry out and lose their viability before warm weather stimulates germination. Black oak seedlings may die back for various reasons leaving the root to generate new shoots; thus root systems can be 10 to 20 years older than the tops.

A deep taproot (straight vertical primary root) and wide-spreading lateral roots develop which is one reason for the tree's prevalence on our dry upland sites. Trees are moderately resistant to fire. Small oaks will be top-killed by fire but sprout from their root crowns, while larger trees can withstand low-severity surface fire because of thicker basal bark.

Many wildlife species eat black oak acorns including squirrels, mice, voles, white-tailed deer, and wild turkey. Trunk cavities in live black oaks can provide bird nesting sites.

Gary R. Sanford

SANDY POND
CONSERVATION AREA

View of Little Sandy Pond and its shoreline.

Sandy Pond Conservation area is accessed from Buck Island Road in West Yarmouth, between Higgins Crowell Road and Town Brook Road. The trail head is located at Little Sandy Pond behind the developed recreation areas, and trails traverse both the conservation area and adjacent Water Department land as shown in Figure 5. As displayed, the site covers roughly 90 acres, and is about 3.3 miles (5.3 km) south of Cape Cod Bay, and 1.5 miles (2.4 km) north of Lewis Bay.

The "Geologic Map of Cape Cod and the Islands, Massachusetts" shows site surficial geology as almost entirely Harwich Outwash Plain Deposits. One small area of marsh and swamp deposits intrude slightly from the west. Harwich outwash plain deposits are mostly gravelly sand with localized deposits of silt and clay.

Little Sandy Pond is a kettle hole formed from a block of glacial ice that was surrounded by sediments. Upon melting, a depression was left that filled with water. The pond's elevation is at about 10 feet. Added contour elevations on Figure 5 show how elevations rise roughly 20 feet to the north, east, and south. The outlet stream, Town Brook, slopes gently to the west, and eventually feeds into Baxter Grist Mill Pond along Route 28.

The Natural Resources Conservation Service has mapped Carver coarse sand, Freetown and Swansea mucks, (coastal lowland, 0 to 1 percent slopes), and Freetown coarse sand (0 to 3 percent slopes, sanded surface) soils on site. Excluding the pond, Carver coarse sand, an upland soil, covers about 85% of the site.

The Carver unit is composed of deep coarse-textured soil that is excessively well drained, and has very rapid permeabilities both in the subsoil and substratum. Soil water holding capacity is low, and depth to the seasonal high groundwater table exceeds 6 feet (2 m). Carver soils tend to be droughty, and, as a result, seedling mortality may be exacerbated.

The "Soil Survey of Barnstable County, Massachusetts" identifies the most common trees on Carver soil as pitch pine, scrub oak, and white oak, and states: "Generally, these trees are of poor quality and seldom attain heights of more than 25 feet."

Freetown and/or Swansea mucks are associated with Town Brook, and extend from the pond to the west off-site. Freetown soil has muck and peat to a depth of 65 inches (1.65 m) or more; Swansea soil has muck to a depth of about 36 inches (.9 m). Muck is highly decomposed organic matter; peat is largely undecomposed organic matter. These soils are similar in having moderate or moderately rapid permeabilities in the organic layers, very high water holding capacity, and seasonal high water tables at or near the surface for most of the year.

DEP has mapped 5 wetland areas on the site as shown in Figure 6. All have been characterized as wooded swamps with varying amounts of deciduous versus evergreen tree canopies ranging from almost totally deciduous, to mixed, to almost totally evergreen (see Figure 6). The wetland located on the west edge of the site (see Figure 6A) is located within marsh and swamp deposits, and within the Freetown and/or Swansea mucks soil map unit. Common trees occurring in wetlands include red maple (*Acer rubrum*), tupelo (*Nyssa sylvatica*), and pitch pine (*Pinus rigida*). A few Atlantic white cedar trees (*Chamaecyparis thyoides*) can be seen scattered along the pond's edge, and a nice stand of the tree is located within the most western wetland (see Figure 6A).

Upland vegetation is dominated by pitch pine and oaks (*Quercus spp.*), with the small woody plants, black huckleberry (*Gaylussacia baccata*) and lowbush blueberry (*Vaccinium angustifolium* and *V. pallidum*), common. Table 3 lists plant species observed along the trails.

Figure 5. Portion of USGS quadrangle showing part of the Sandy Pond Conservation Area. Contour interval = 10 ft. Quadrangle from Bureau of Geographic Information, Commonwealth of Massachusetts, Executive Office of Technology and Security Services. Trails from Town of Yarmouth Trail Map.

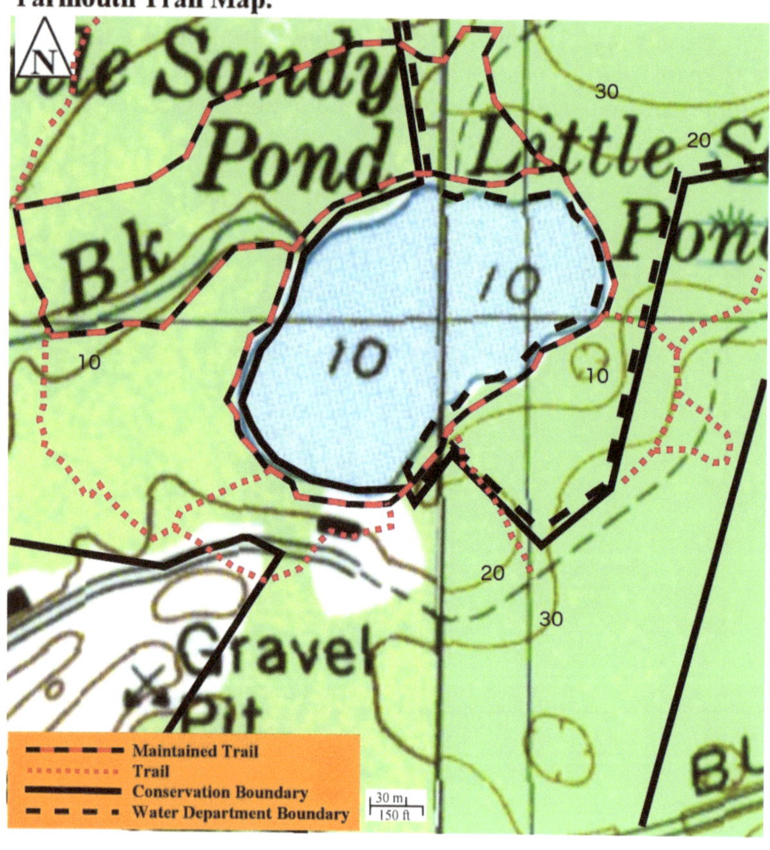

Figure 6A. **Orthophotograph of Sandy Pond Conservation Area.** **DEP wetland boundary from Bureau of Geographic Information, Commonwealth of Massachusetts, Executive Office of Technology and Security Services.** **Trails from Town of Yarmouth Trail Map.**

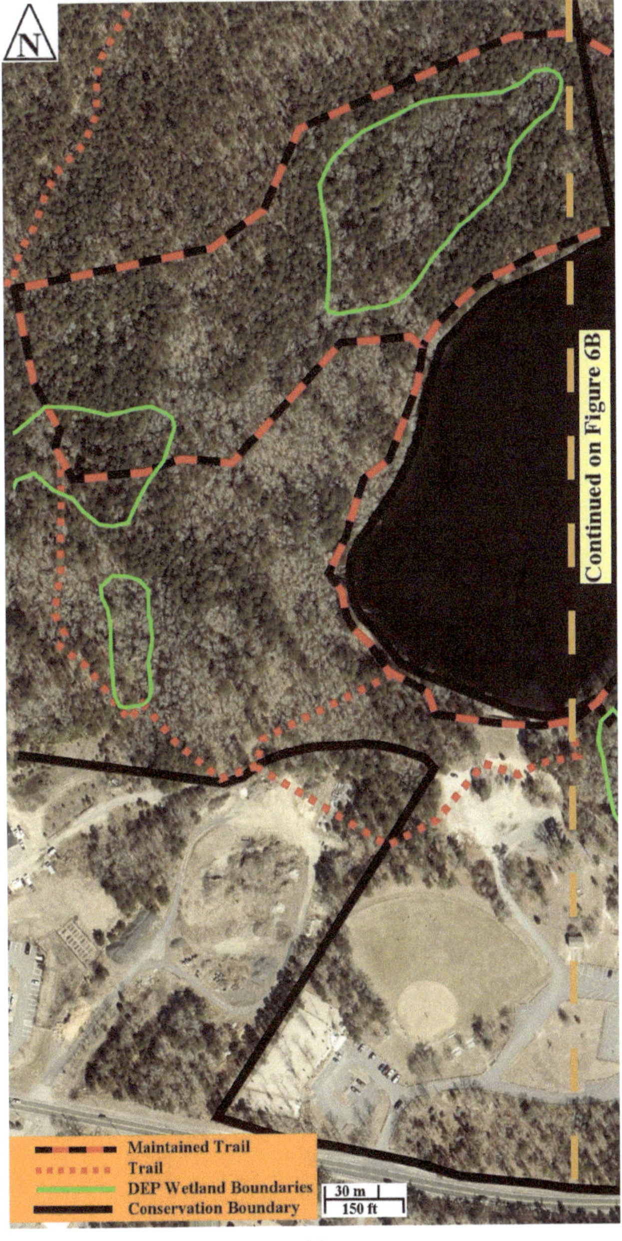

Figure 6B.   Orthophotograph of Sandy Pond Conservation Area.   DEP wetland boundary from Bureau of Geographic Information, Commonwealth of Massachusetts, Executive Office of Technology and Security Services. Trails from Town of Yarmouth Trail Map.

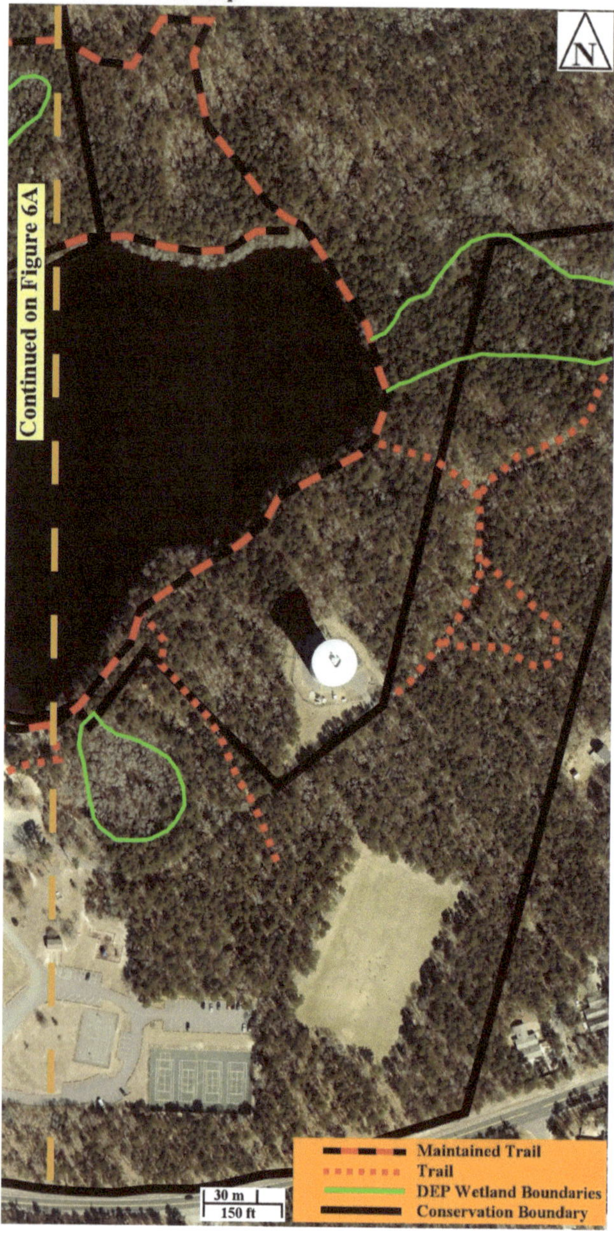

Table 3. Checklist of species noted along Sandy Pond Conservation Area trails.

✓	Scientific Name	Common Name	Wetland Status[1]	Growth Habit[2]
	Quercus coccinea Münchh.	scarlet oak	upland[3]	Tree
	Quercus velutina Lam.	black oak	upland[3]	Tree
	Pinus rigida Mill.	pitch pine	FACU	Tree
	Pinus strobus L.	eastern white pine	FACU	Tree
	Populus grandidentata Michx.	big-tooth aspen	FACU	Tree
	Quercus alba L.	white oak	FACU	Tree
	Quercus rubra L.	northern red oak	FACU	Tree
	Acer rubrum L.	red maple	FAC	Tree
	Betula populifolia Marshall	gray birch	FAC	Tree
	Nyssa sylvatica Marsh.	tupelo	FAC	Tree
	Chamaecyparis thyoides (L.) Britton, Sterns & Poggenb.	Atlantic white cedar	OBL	Tree
	Quercus ilicifolia Wangenh.	bear oak	upland[3]	Shrub/Tree
	Gaylussacia baccata (Wangenh.) K. Koch	black huckleberry	FACU	Shrub
	Ilex opaca Alton	American holly	FACU	Shrub/Tree

✓	Scientific Name	Common Name	Wetland Status[1]	Growth Habit[2]
	Lonicera morrowii A. Gray	**Morrow's honeysuckle**	**FACU**	**Shrub**
	Prunus serotina Ehrh.	**black cherry**	**FACU**	**Shrub/Tree**
	Vaccinium stamineum L.	**deerberry**	**FACU**	**Shrub**
	Amelanchier canadensis (L.) Medik.	**Canadian serviceberry**	**FAC**	**Shrub/Tree**
	Morella pensylvanica (Mirbel) Kartesz	**northern bayberry**	**FAC**	**Shrub/Tree**
	Clethra alnifolia L.	**sweet pepper bush**	**FAC**	**Shrub**
	Kalmia angustifolia L.	**sheep laurel**	**FAC**	**Shrub**
	Smilax rotundifolia L.	**horsebrier**	**FAC**	**Shrub/Vine**
	Eubotrys racemosus (L.) Nutt.	**swamp doghobble; Fetterbush**	**FACW**	**Shrub**
	Ilex glabra (L.) Gray	**inkberry**	**FACW**	**Shrub**
	Rhododendron viscosum (L.) Torr.	**swamp azalea**	**FACW**	**Shrub**
	Vaccinium corymbosum L.	**highbush blueberry**	**FACW**	**Shrub**
	Chimaphila umbellata (L.) W.P.C. Barton	**pipsissewa**	**upland[3]**	**Subshrub**
	Comptonia peregrina (L.) J.M. Coult.	**sweet fern**	**upland[3]**	**Shrub/ Subshrub**

✓	Scientific Name	Common Name	Wetland Status[1]	Growth Habit[2]
	Vaccinium pallidum Aiton	early lowbush blueberry	upland[3]	Subshrub
	Gaultheria procumbens L.	wintergreen, eastern teaberry	FACU	Shrub/ Subshrub
	Vaccinium angustifolium Aiton	late lowbush blueberry	FACU	Shrub/ Subshrub
	Toxicodendron radicans (L.) Kuntze	eastern poison ivy	FAC	Forb/herb Shrub Subshrub Vine
	Aralia nudicaulis L.	wild sarsaparilla	FACU	Forb/herb Subshrub
	Maianthemum canadense Desf.	Canada mayflower	FACU	Forb/herb
	Polygonum cuspidatum Siebold & Zucc.	Japanese knotweed	FACU	Forb/herb Subshrub
	Pteridium aquilinum (L.) Kuhn	brackenfern	FACU	Forb/herb
	Trientalis borealis Raf.	starflower	FAC	Forb/herb
	Osmunda cinnamomea L.	cinnamon fern	FACW	Forb/herb
	Thelypteris simulata (Davenport) Nieuwl.	bog fern	FACW	Forb/herb
	Nymphaea odorata Aiton	American white waterlily	OBL	Forb/herb

✓	Scientific Name	Common Name	Wetland Status[1]	Growth Habit[2]
	Carex pensylvanica Lam	Pennsylvania sedge	upland[3]	Graminoid
	Sphagnum L.	sphagnum	wetland	Nonvascular

[1]See Appendix 1 [2]See Appendix 2. [3]Not listed on the National Wetland Plant List.

Additional Ecological Information: Atlantic White Cedar

Atlantic white cedar (*Chamaecyparis thyoides*) has a narrow spike-like form, reaching 50 or 75 feet (15 or 23 m) in height with a crown only 10 or 20 feet (3 or 8 m) in diameter. The gray to red-brown bark is thin and fibrous; leaves are scale like, and 1/16 to 1/8 inch (1.6 to 3.2 mm) long. Branchlets form more or less flat fern like sprays. Trees are monoecious (male and female cones are produced on a single tree), Female cones are small [about 1/4 inch (6.4 mm) in diameter], usually have 4 or 5 scales, and each produces 5 to 15 laterally winged seeds.

Atlantic white cedar may be confused with red cedar (*Juniperus virginiana)*, and can be distinguished by its habitat affinity. *Chamaecyparis thyoides* is usually found in wetlands, while red cedar usually grows in uplands. Atlantic white cedar leaves are of one type, small and scaly with white margins. Red cedar leaves are of two types, scale and awl-like, and they lack the white margins.

Chamaecyparis thyoides grows in a narrow range of environments resulting in a patchy distribution. It occurs within a coastal belt 50 to 130 miles (80 to 210 km) wide along the Atlantic and Gulf coasts from Maine to southern Mississippi. The tree, rarely found in uplands, is a dominant in very wet forested wetlands, and can be common or co-dominant in red maple wetlands.

Seeds need light and continuous moisture for germination, and can remain viable in the forest litter for many years. Although a seedling begins growth with a very short tap root, an extensive system of lateral roots develops resulting in a shallow root system that is confined above the water table. The pit and mound micro-relief (small hummocks a foot or so high and several feet in diameter mirrored by small depressions) found in many wetlands can be critical to seedling survival, since the very short tap root must be near the water table, and yet the seedling can dry out and die on the slightly higher portions of a mound.

Wind pollination occurs in the spring, and the cones are mature by the end of the first growing season. Most seeds are shed and dispersed by wind in the fall, but shedding can continue throughout the winter with cones opening during good weather and closing when significant rain occurs. Seed production is prolific, with reports of 9 million per acre being produced.

Although trees are intermediate in shade tolerance, seedlings don't do well with tree or shrub overgrowth. Because of the shallow rooting habit, individual trees are quite susceptible to wind-throw, however dense stands of trees form a unit more resistant to high winds. High winds and other factors, such as fire, flooding, and clear-cutting, can lead to dense even aged stands that usually do not exceed 200 years in age. Growth in height essentially ceases after about 100 years, but trees can be long-lived with some being reported to be 1,000 years old.

Although fire readily kills adult trees, seedling establishment is largely dependent on short interval fires which produce open conditions. Seeds present in the peaty wet soils may remain undamaged if the fire is only of moderate severity, and may germinate to reestablish trees. Off-site seed can be carried onto a burn area by animals or water. A crop of seedlings and young trees can be a favorite food source for deer, and browsing can be a significant mortality factor. Mice may occasionally browse stems and can girdle seedlings.

APPENDIX 1

The "wetland status" used in Tables 1, 2, and 3 are obtained from ratings listed in the "2016 National Wetland Plant List". Short indicator rating definitions, shown below, are taken from Lichvar, R. et al., July 2012. Lichvar et al. also provide longer definitions which identify wetland features and provide plant examples.

OBL (Obligate Wetland Plants)—Almost always occur in wetlands.

FACW (Facultative Wetland Plants)—Usually occur in wetlands, but may occur in non-wetlands.

FAC (Facultative Wetland Plants)—Occur in wetlands and non-wetlands.

FACU (Facultative Upland Plants)—Usually occur in non-wetlands, but may occur in wetlands.

UPL (Upland Plants)—Almost never occur in wetlands.

Gary R. Sanford

APPENDIX 2

Growth habits and definitions are taken from:
https://plants.usda.gov/core/profile.

PLANTS Description	PLANTS Definition	Note
Forb/herb	Vascular plant without significant woody tissue above or at the ground. Forbs and herbs may be annual, biennial, or perennial but always lack significant thickening by secondary woody growth and have perennating buds borne at or below the ground surface. In PLANTS, graminoids are excluded but ferns, horsetails, lycopods, and whisk-ferns are included.	Applies to vascular plants only. Federal Geographic Data Committee (FGDC) definition includes graminoids, forbs, and ferns.
Graminoid	Grass or grass-like plant, including grasses (Poaceae), sedges (Cyperaceae), rushes (Juncaceae), arrow-grasses (Juncaginaceae), and quillworts (*Isoetes*).	Applies to vascular plants only. An herb in the FGDC classification.
Lichenous	Organism generally recognized as a single "plant" that consists of a fungus and an alga or cyanobacterium living in symbiotic association. Often attached to solid objects such as rocks or living or dead wood rather than soil.	Applies to lichens only, which are not true plants.
Nonvascular	Nonvascular, terrestrial green plant, including mosses, hornworts, and liverworts. Always herbaceous, often	Applies to non-vascular plants only; in PLANTS system this is groups HN (Hornworts), LV

PLANTS Description	PLANTS Definition	Note
	attached to solid objects such as rocks or living or dead wood rather than soil.	(Liverworts), and MS (Mosses).
Shrub	Perennial, multi-stemmed woody plant that is usually less than 4 to 5 meters (13 to 16 feet) in height. Shrubs typically have several stems arising from or near the ground, but may be taller than 5 meters or single-stemmed under certain environmental conditions.	Applies to vascular plants only.
Subshrub	Low-growing shrub usually under 0.5 m (1.5 feet) tall, never exceeding 1 meter (3 feet) tall at maturity.	Applies to vascular plants only. A dwarf-shrub in the FGDC classification.
Tree	Perennial, woody plant with a single stem (trunk), normally greater than 4 to 5 meters (13 to 16 feet) in height; under certain environmental conditions, some tree species may develop a multi-stemmed or short growth form (less than 4 meters or 13 feet in height).	Applies to vascular plants only.
Vine	Twining/climbing plant with relatively long stems, can be woody or herbaceous.	Applies to vascular plants only. FGDC classification considers woody vines to be shrubs and herbaceous vines to be herbs.

APPENDIX 3

Comparison of some characteristics among Carter, Plymouth, Barnstable, and Nantucket soils. (taken from Web Soil Survey. USDA Natural Resources Conservation Service).

	Carver coarse sand	Plymouth loamy coarse sand	Barnstable sandy loam	Nantucket sandy loam
Setting	Landform: Moraines, outwash plains	Landform: Moraines	Landform: Moraines	Landform: Moraines
Natural drainage class	Excessively drained	Excessively drained	Well drained	Well drained
Typical profile	Oi - 0 to 2 inches: slightly decomposed plant material Oe - 2 to 3 inches: moderately decomposed plant material A - 3 to 7 inches: coarse sand E - 7 to 10 inches: coarse sand Bw1 - 10 to 15 inches: coarse sand Bw2 - 15 to 28 inches: coarse sand BC - 28 to 32 inches: coarse sand C - 32 to 67 inches: coarse sand	H1 - 0 to 3 inches: loamy coarse sand H2 - 3 to 29 inches: gravelly loamy coarse sand H3 - 29 to 64 inches: gravelly coarse sand	H1 - 0 to 1 inches: sandy loam H2 - 1 to 23 inches: sandy loam H3 - 23 to 64 inches: coarse sand	H1 - 0 to 5 inches: sandy loam H2 - 5 to 27 inches: sandy loam H3 - 27 to 64 inches: loam
Frequency of flooding / ponding	Frequency of flooding: None Frequency of ponding: None	Frequency of flooding: None Frequency of ponding: None	Frequency of flooding: None Frequency of ponding: None	Frequency of flooding: None Frequency of ponding: None
Capacity of the most limiting layer to transmit water (Ksat)	Moderately high to very high (1.42 to 14.17 in/hr)	High to very high (6.00 to 20.00 in/hr)	High (2.00 to 6.00 in/hr)	Moderately low to moderately high (0.06 to 0.60 in/hr)
Available water storage in profile	Low (about 4.3 inches)	Low (about 3.0 inches)	Low (about 4.0 inches)	Low (about 3.6 inches)
Depth to water table	More than 80 inches	More than 80 inches	More than 80 inches	About 24 to 30 inches

Location of soils within the Bud Carter Conservation area..

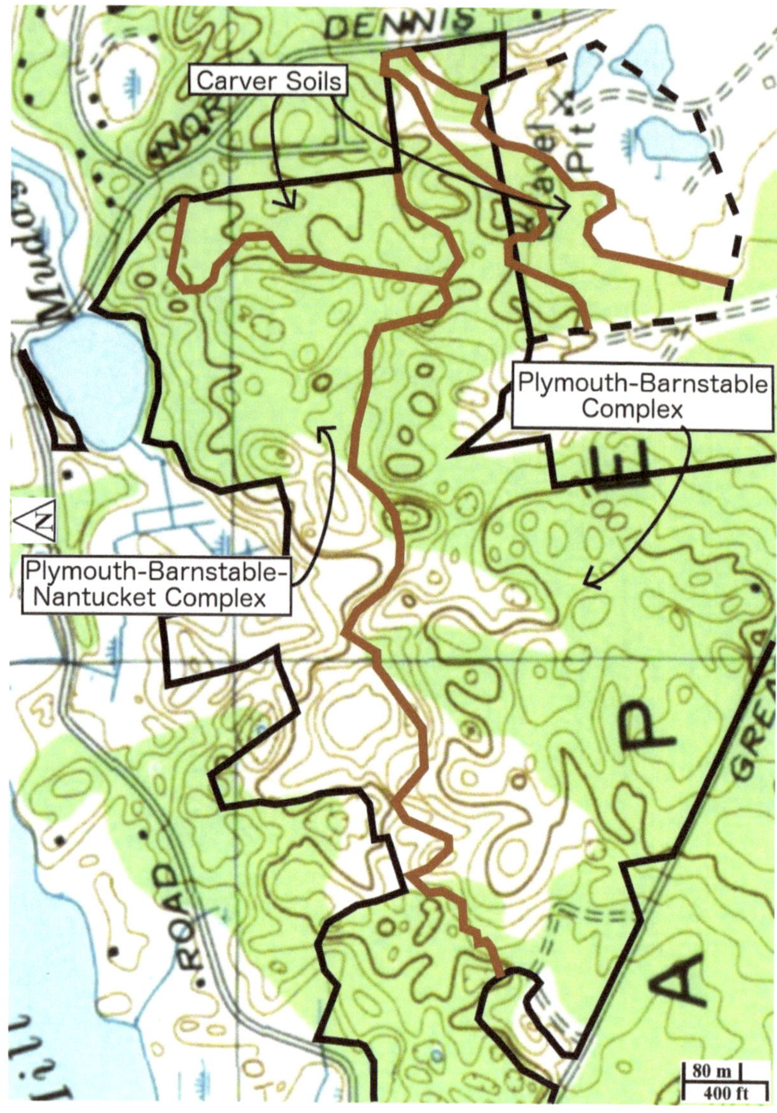

INFORMATION SOURCES

Carey, Jennifer H. 1992. Quercus velutina. In: Fire Effects In- formation System, [Online]. U.S. Department of Agriculture, Forest Service, Rocky Mountain Research Station, Fire Sciences Laboratory (Producer). 2012, December 7
Available:
https://www.feis-crs.org/feis/

Fletcher, P. 1993. Soil Survey of Barnstable County, Massachusetts. Technical report of the U.S. Department of Agriculture, Soil Conservation Service.
Available:
https://www.nrcs.usda.gov/wps/portal/nrcs/detail/ma/soils/surveys/?cid=nrcs144p2_013984

Laderman, Aimlee D. 1989. THE ECOLOGY OF ATLANTIC WHITE CEDAR WETLANDS: A COMMUNITY PROFILE. US Fish and Wildlife Service. Biological Report 85(7.21)
Available:
http://aquaticcommons.org/8862/1/white_cedar_community_profile.pdf

Lichvar, R.W., D.L. Banks, W.N. Kirchner, and N.C. Melvin. 2016. The National Wetland Plant List: 2016 wetland ratings. Phytoneuron 2016-30: 1-17. Published 28 April 2016. ISSN 2153 733X.
Available:
http://wetland-plants.usace.army.mil/nwpl_static/v33/home/home.html

Lichvar, R. W., N. C. Melvin, M. L. Butterwick, & W. N. Kirchner. July 2012. National Wetland Plant List; Indicator Rating Definitions. U.S. Army Corps of Engineers, Engineer Research and Development Center, Cold Regions Research and Engineering Laboratory, Hanover, NH, and BONAP, Chapel Hill, NC. ERDC/CRREL TN-12-1.
Available:
https://www.fws.gov/wetlands/documents/National-Wetland-Plant-List-Indicator-Rating-Definitions.pdf

Little, S. and P. W. Garrett. 1990. Chamaecyparis thyoides (L.) B.S. P. Atlantic White-Cedar. IN: R. M. Burns, and B. H. Honkala, (tech. Coords.). Silvics of North America 1. Conifers; 2. Hardwoods. Publication: Agriculture Handbook 654, U.S. Dept. of Agriculture, Forest Service.
Available:
https://www.srs.fs.usda.gov/pubs/misc/ag_654/volume_1/chamaecyparis/thyoides.htm

NRCS Plant Guide: LEATHERLEAF Chamaedaphne calyculata (L.) Moench. USDA NRCS National Plant Data Center & the Biota of North America Program.
Available: **https://plants.usda.gov/plantguide/pdf/pg_chca2.pdf**

Oldale, R.N. and R.A. Barlow. 1986. Geologic map of Cape Cod and the Islands, Massachusetts. U.S. Geological Survey, IMAP 1763
Available:
https://doi.org/10.3133/i1763

Pavek, Diane S. 1993. Chamaedaphne calyculata. In: Fire Effects Information System, [Online]. U.S. Department of Agriculture, Forest Service, Rocky Mountain Research Station, Fire Sciences Laboratory (Producer).
Available:
https://www.feis-crs.org/feis/

Sander, I. L. 1990. Quercus velutina Lam. Black Oak. IN: R. M. Burns and B. H. Honkala, (tech. Coords.). Silvics of North America 1. Conifers; 2. Hardwoods. Publication: Agriculture Handbook 654, U.S. Dept. of Agriculture, Forest Service. Available:
https://www.srs.fs.usda.gov/pubs/misc/ag_654/volume_2/quercus/velutina.htm

Stein, John, D. Binion, & R. Acciavatti. 2003. Field Guide to Native Oak Species of Eastern North America, USDA Forest Service, FHTET-2003-01.
Available:
https://www.fs.fed.us/foresthealth/technology/pdfs/fieldguide.pdf

Tirmenstein, D. A. 1991. Chamaecyparis thyoides. In: Fire Effects Information System, [Online]. U.S. Department of Agriculture, Forest Service, Rocky Mountain Research Station, Fire Sciences Laboratory (Producer). (2012, February 15).
Available:
https://www.feis-crs.org/feis/

Town of Yarmouth. Trail Map. Bud Carter Conservation Area.
Available:
https://www.yarmouth.ma.us/1672/Bud-Carter-Conservation-Area
https://www.yarmouth.ma.us/DocumentCenter/View/9925/BudCarter?bidId=

Town of Yarmouth. Trail Map. Horse Pond Conservation Area.
Available:
https://www.yarmouth.ma.us/1674/Horse-Pond-Conservation-Area
https://www.yarmouth.ma.us/DocumentCenter/View/9926/HorsePond?bidId=

Town of Yarmouth. Trail Map. Sandy Pond Conservation Area.
Available:
https://www.yarmouth.ma.us/1677/Sandy-Pond-Conservation-Area
https://www.yarmouth.ma.us/DocumentCenter/View/9921/SandyPond?bidId=

USDA Natural Resources Conservation Services. Fact Sheet, Atlantic White Cedar, Chamaecyparis thyoides (L.) B.S.P.
Available:
https://plants.usda.gov/factsheet/pdf/fs_chth2.pdf

USGS. GEOLOGIC HISTORY OF CAPE COD, MASSACHUSETTS
Available:
https://pubs.usgs.gov/gip/capecod/index.html

Web Soil Survey. USDA Natural Resources Conservation Service – Soils
Available:
https://www.nrcs.usda.gov/wps/portal/nrcs/main/soils/survey/

ABOUT THE AUTHOR

Gary Sanford spent his youth on a ranch near Sebastopol, California, where agricultural products included eggs, apples, and cherries. After obtaining a Ph.D. in botany from the University of California, Davis campus, he moved to Massachusetts in the early 1970s, and has spent the last 45+ years in New England. Most of this time was spent working as an environmental consultant and botanist. The past few years have been devoted to non-fiction writing. He co-authored "The Ecology of Common Woody Plants of Cape Cod" and "Chester: A Buddy Forever". He authored "Three Cape Cod Botanical Walks In Dennis, MA".

(email - garysanford43@gmail.com)